Creative
Embroidery
Today

Olive Pounds

Formerly Head of the Needlework Department, Shirley Warren School, Southampton
and Chief Examiner in Embroidery for the Certificate of Secondary Education

Nelson

Thomas Nelson and Sons Ltd.
36 Park Street London W1Y 4DE
P.O. Box 18123 Nairobi Kenya
Thomas Nelson (Australia) Ltd.
597 Little Collins Street Melbourne 3000
Thomas Nelson and Sons (Canada) Ltd.
81 Curlew Drive Don Mills Ontario
Thomas Nelson (Nigeria) Ltd.
P.O. Box 336 Apapa Lagos
Thomas Nelson and Sons (South Africa)
(Proprietary) Ltd.
51 Commissioner Street Johannesburg

© Olive Pounds 1972
First published 1972
Second impression 1974
ISBN 0 17 438026 7

Photoset by BAS Printers Limited,
Wallop, Hampshire

Printed by The Camelot Press Ltd,
London and Southampton

Contents

Preface

This book has been written in response to many requests for guidance for young students attempting embroidery at a serious level perhaps for the first time. The reader is guided through the difficulties of designing by the simplest methods, and is then shown a variety of stitches most commonly in use. After this come details of other techniques used in embroidery and notes on examination techniques to help students studying for G.C.E. and C.S.E. Finally there is a selection of questions from recent examination papers.

O.P.

Acknowledgements

Grateful thanks are due to the following for permission to use material on the pages indicated:
The Coats Sewing Group—diagrams on pp 33 to 49; The Nottingham Handcraft Company—photos on pp 26 and 29; The Victoria and Albert Museum—photos on pp 54 and 62; Mr. H. Beasley for all remaining photos.

Illustrations by Gillian Zeiner; diagrams by Colin Rattray Associates.
The cover picture shows a radiograph of a shell, reproduced by courtesy of United Press International.

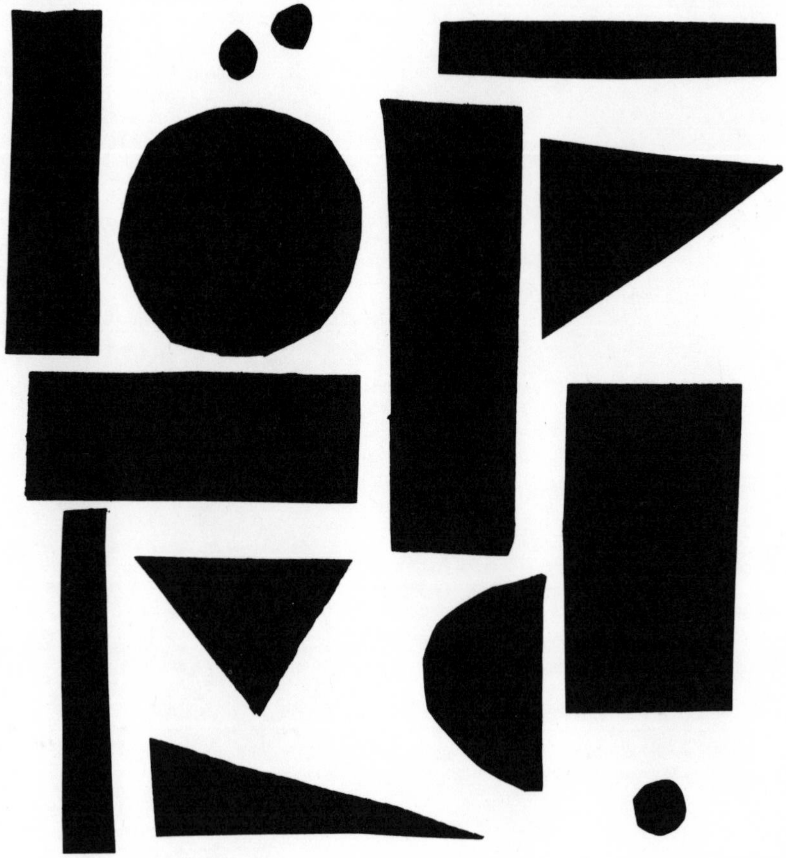

Design 1

There are seven basic motifs of design.

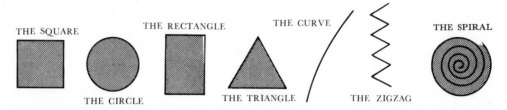

THE SQUARE   THE RECTANGLE   THE CURVE   THE SPIRAL

THE CIRCLE   THE TRIANGLE   THE ZIGZAG

Any of these motifs can be used separately or together in any kind of combination to build up a design. Cut out the shapes in several different sizes, preferably in black paper, and lay them on to a sheet of white paper. Move them about, overlap them, use only one shape or more than one and gradually you will get the feel for design.

For a three-dimensional exercise, use matchboxes and rounds of cardboard cut from sweet cartons. The matchboxes can be used flat, upright or on the side, each giving a different dimension. The rounds of cardboard can be cut through to give semi-circles or crescents. When you are satisfied with the layout, draw what you have made. The drawing will be flat, as fabric is flat, and you will then be able to think of how you will interpret it in fabric and thread.

For a free design, make several ink blots close together. With the paper flat on the table, and using a drinking straw, blow the wet blots, making the ink run in various directions. When the ink is dry, the spaces in the design may be coloured for a change of effect.

Further interesting designs can be made by brushing clean water on to the paper and dropping on one or more blots of ink or paint. The inks will spread to give a tie and dye effect.

Small sections of these free designs may be chosen for enlargement and working.

Seeing things

There is an infinite variety of design in the world around you. If you will walk about with 'seeing eyes', on one day perhaps looking only for circles, you will see such things as wheels, clock faces, pretty plates, coal chute covers, etc. When you cut an apple or any other rounded fruit in half you will have a circle with an interesting design within it.

Start looking for curves and you will see handles of all shapes and sizes keyhole covers, the tops of windows, and architectural mouldings.

I

The triangular shape will bring your eyes looking upwards to the roofs of buildings with their attractive outline filled in with nicely shaped tiles, or to road signs and the advertisements. Iron railings are often made of a combination of curves and straight lines.

You will soon realise that shape and design are all about you, so keep a small notebook with you and make sketches of anything interesting to add to your file. Shoes are a source of constantly changing fashion; the fastenings and forms of decoration could well make an interesting study.

Your file should consist of a folder in which to keep sheets of sketches or cut-outs from magazines, newspapers, etc: you will also need a pocket file in which to keep your templates.

A template is a shape cut in strong paper, card, wood or metal. It is used to transfer a shape to a design sheet, or directly on to the fabric. A collection of templates is a very valuable part of your equipment and should be added to constantly, particularly if you are entering for an examination.

You may think that you cannot design because you are not very good at drawing, but you can certainly use scissors and you can use a pencil so that designing is not impossible, as you will see.

3

4

Cut paper shapes

Take a piece of paper and fold it in half, then starting from the folded edge cut any shape you like, perhaps a curve shaped like a leaf. When you have finished cutting, open out the paper and you will have a shape which is exactly the same on either side of the centre crease line. You have now made a template. Place this template on a sheet of paper and draw round it; take away the template and you will have the first part of a design on your drawing sheet. Use the template again and again, perhaps at different angles or overlapping.

If you cut out seven leaf shapes all exactly alike, you could place them on top of each other in your hand and hold them like a pack of cards. Fan them out as though you were playing a card game, lay them on a sheet of paper as they are and you will have the outline of a flower head to which you can add a few stamens, a circle for the calyx, and straight or curved lines for the stem.

If you now pick up the piece of paper from which you cut your first template and open this out, you will see that the space itself is an interesting shape bordered by a plain outline. This whole shape is again a template in itself.

If you pleat the paper and cut through all the folds, when you open it out you will have a repeat design.

An interesting exercise in colour can be enjoyed by cutting out the shapes in coloured tissue paper and seeing how effectively you can arrange them.

Related shapes

Another simple but effective way of creating a design is by the use of the related shape.

For a first exercise cut out several circles in black paper. From each circle cut out a segment, making a different shape each time. Paste the circle on to white paper and put the segment in close proximity, and the relationship between the two will be clearly seen.

Repeat the exercise using four of the basic motifs of design. To soften the edges of the straight-lined motifs, the corners may be torn off.

Extend the exercise further by cutting in either straight lines or curves right across the basic shape. Number each section, in order.

On a sheet of contrasting paper lay the shapes matched together again. Then start moving the shapes away from each other, and immediately you will notice that the space between them is related to the shapes themselves.

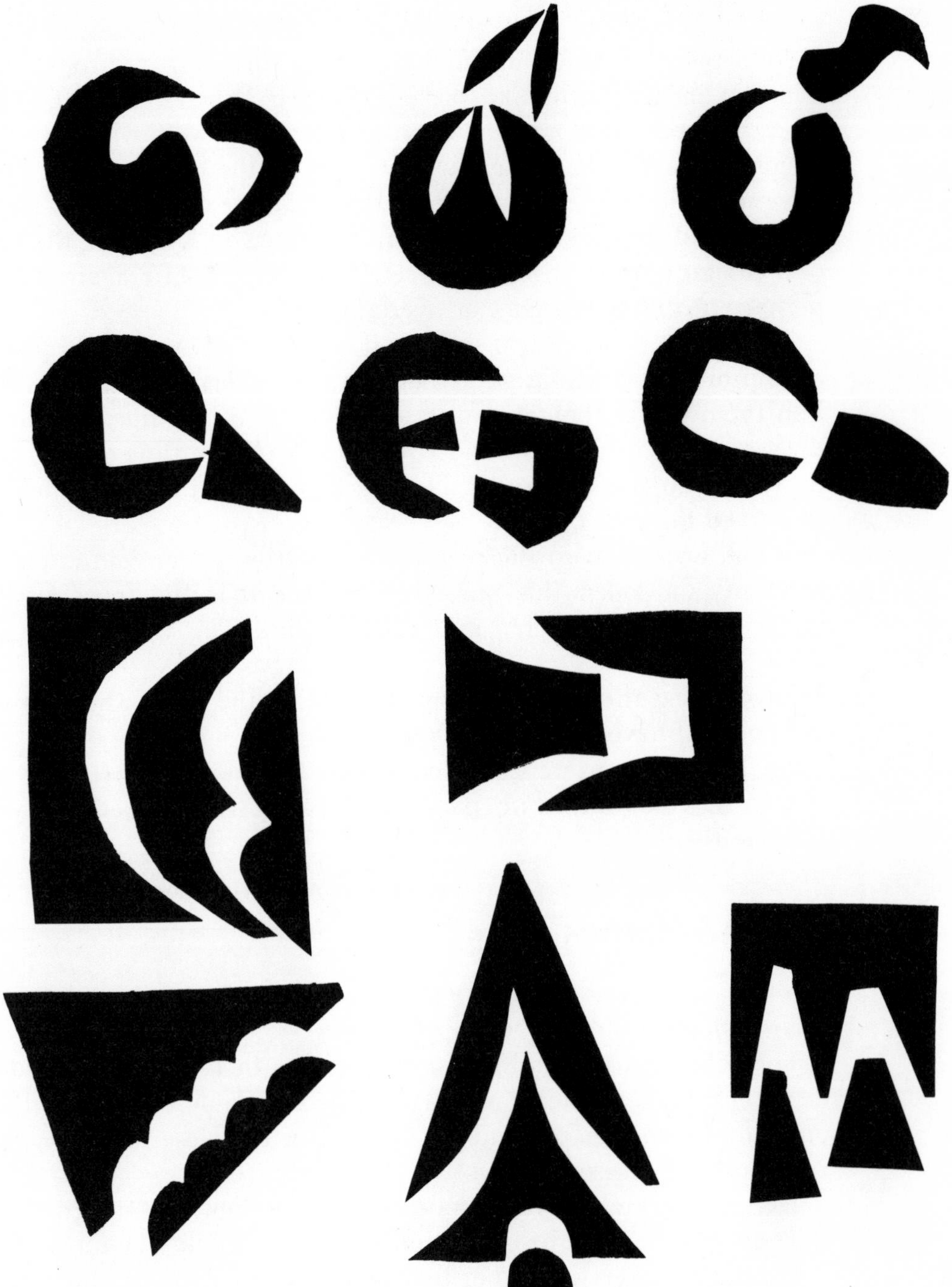

When making up such a design either the space or the shape may be embroidered, couched or appliquéd. There are many possibilities which you will be able to discover for yourself.

Once you start you will be able to see related shapes all around you. If you take a close look at the letters of the alphabet as used in advertising you will see that the artist may have used related shapes for emphasis. This medium of impact is used a great deal in magazines, so with a little effort you could build up a very interesting file on related shapes.

The moving line

A line can be either straight or curved, it can be thick or thin, it can be broken or continuous.

Take a length of wool or string and toss it in the air, and it will fall into a natural shape. Hold the wool or string in the palm of your hand and drop it on to a contrasting sheet of paper or fabric. The wool will fall quite naturally into a moving line which you would have found difficult to 'see' for yourself. Pin the 'line' into the position in which it fell and draw round it or couch it directly on to the fabric using this natural line as the basis for a design. Make use of the related shapes between the moving line for enriching the fabric either with embroidery stitches or with collage.

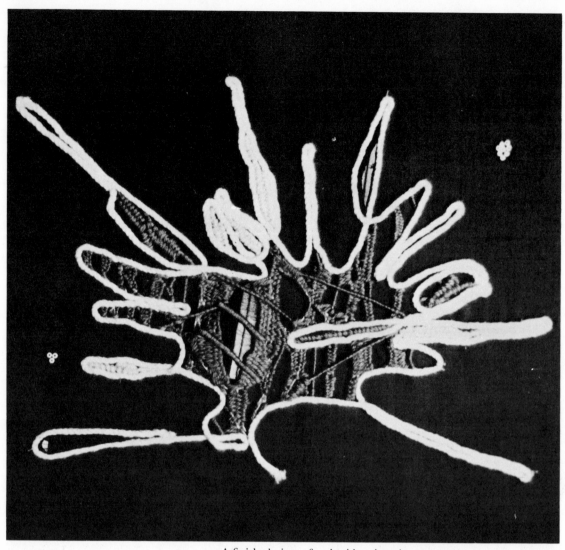

A finished piece of embroidery based on a name. LINDA WRIGHT (15).

The written word is a moving line. Use a felt tip pen and write your own name, varying the size and the direction of the letters, and turning the paper round using the other hand as you write. You will have wide or narrow spaces between the curves and straight lines—in fact a very interesting design which could be used as the basis of a piece of embroidery. Some parts of the design could be blocked in, other parts could be outlined or thickened to create a feeling of texture, or richly embroidered. The finished embroidery would not be a name but a composition in movement. Parts of the design might be so interesting that they could be used as repeat designs.

Commercial art

If you look at advertisements from the design angle you will notice that particularly with the style of lettering the artist makes use of the related shape. Many advertisements when looked at only as line drawings will give an excellent outline for the basis of a piece of work. Boys who do embroidery will see the possibilities of a blueprint for an electronic layout; the London Underground map has design possibilities; the constellations may also give you inspiration, and if you are really out of ideas you will find plenty in a wallpaper book.

Natural forms

Under this heading come

GRASSES   LEAVES   FUNGI   SEED PODS

SHELLS   FEATHERS   TREE BARK   DRIFT WOOD

    Some of these natural forms could be mounted to form a valuable record to which you could with advantage turn to from time to time. Other forms could be sketched as closely as possible to the original for future reference, and rubbings could be taken of others.

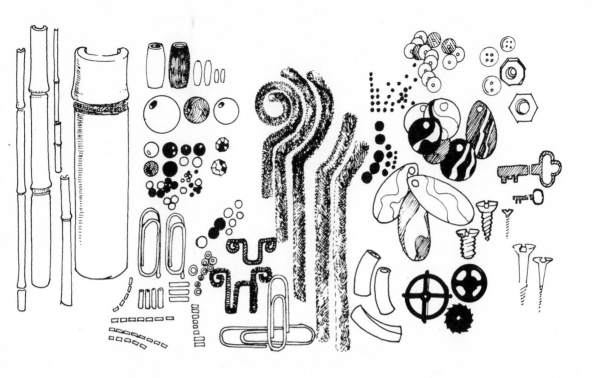

Found and applied objects

When making a collage added interest is often given by applying objects to supplement the stitchery.

A box will be necessary for the storage of found objects. Such articles as beads of all shapes and sizes, pipe cleaners in their various colours, watch wheels, paper clips, metal nuts, short pieces of bamboo cane, small watch keys, furhooks, mirror glass, etc. You will quickly become used to looking at objects with the thought 'I could use that' running through your mind.

Dried grasses, seed pods and other dried materials are best treated with a coat of quick drying enamel and then used after they have dried; this prevents the material from dropping. Small pebbles and tiny sea shells will have their natural colours enhanced if they are given a coat of clear varnish, but they can also be coloured with enamel if a special colour is required.

CLEAR BOSTIK NO. I will stick solid objects to fabrics, and so will Marvin Medium, but if the object is very heavy then it would be advisable to add a few stitches to hold it in place.

COPYDEX will stick fabric to fabric, wood to fabric and paper to fabric.

MARVIN MEDIUM will stick fabric to fabric, solid objects to fabric and most substances to fabric.

WHITE RICE STARCH will stick fabric to fabric, and it has the advantage of not spoiling the fabric when dry or when laundered. It is especially suitable for appliqué work. Pour boiling water on to white rice in a large cup and leave it to cool. Cover the shaped pieces evenly and thinly with the starch (use your fingers to do this), place the starched pieces on the background fabric, cover with tissue paper and press with a warm iron.

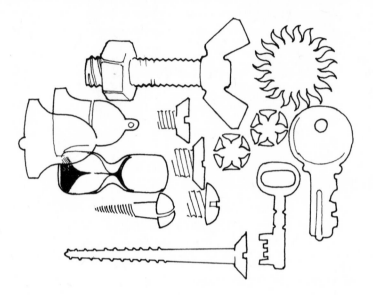

Colour

The human eye is in fact a camera of very high quality, as it photographs for us the things which we see. Not all of these 'cameras' are of the same quality—young people see colour more clearly sometimes than very much older people, so that it can be said that the colour is in the eye of the beholder.

The colour which we see most of in the world around us is green. The grass, the trees, the plants—but these are not all the same green. This difference in colour is called 'hue' in painting but is called 'shade' in fabric. We will talk about shade.

When a series of shades are placed together in ascending or descending order this is called 'tone'.

You could try out an experiment in tone by using shades of one colour in tissue paper, placing them in tonal order as you see them. If you overlap the tissue papers a depth of colour is obtained and this is called a deeper tone.

Look again at the flowers on plants. There are many different coloured flowers yet they all have green stems and leaves. Collect a bunch of different flowers and look carefully at the shades of green; they will often be different but each one will be 'right' for the bright or pale coloured flower which is on its stem.

Now try to do this with fabrics. Find pieces of fabric of as many shades of green as you can. Cut them in half. With one half make a tonal exercise, keep the other half separate and try to find pieces of fabric which will nearly match the colours of the flowers and then put them with the 'right' shades of green. You could mount this exercise to go in your file.

Shade, tone and depth of course apply to all other colours, so do a similar exercise with as many colours as possible.

LIGHT AND DARK

Colours appear to alter when they are used under artificial light, when they are in strong sunlight, and on a dull day. The way a fabric is woven also influences the colour and this is called texture. A smooth fabric gives a clear, sometimes shiny colour; a rough tweed type of fabric gives a deeper, dull look. Some colours denote 'warmth' and some 'coldness'. Collect 'warm' and 'cold' fabrics for your file.

COMPLEMENTARY OR CONTRASTING COLOURS

All colours react to other colours in different ways. When placed together in the same quantity they will either seem 'happy' to be together or the reaction will be quite violent, so that the colours appear to 'quarrel'. From your collection of fabrics choose those which react in this way. Now take small pieces of contrasting or complementary colour fabrics and place these on a larger fabric background, noting the different reactions. Do the exercise again, this time with embroidery threads of all kinds, and again placing the embroidery threads on to the fabrics.

You will begin to understand how colours react towards each other and why it becomes necessary to give much time and thought to the colour content of fabric and thread before starting your embroidery.

Design 2

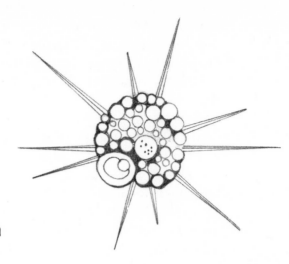

Recording the design

TRACING

You will need a pencil with a good sharp point and some sheets of strong tracing paper.

In Botany and Biology books there are many interesting designs, and if you choose a book which has good line drawings instead of coloured plates the design will be much clearer in outline. Most libraries keep a good supply of such books, so a wide choice of design should be possible.

To trace you must lay the tracing paper over the design and draw carefully over the outline which can be seen through the paper.

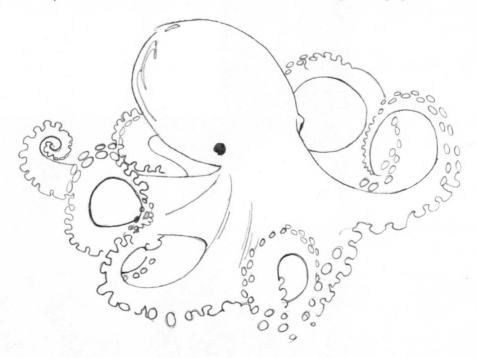

RUBBINGS

Another way to record designs is to make rubbings and this is particularly useful for recording leaf shapes etc. This is what you do.

Take a sheet of thin plain paper and a wax crayon or thick pencil. Place a leaf underside upwards on a flat surface and cover it with the plain paper. The paper should be larger than the leaf. Scribble gently with the crayon over the paper until the shape of the leaf and its markings clearly show. Cut the paper to the shape of the leaf about 2 cm outside the actual rubbing.

You could make a collection of rubbings for your folder, arranging them according to their shape. As well as leaves you could try tree bark, tyres etc. By pouring coloured inks over these rubbings an interesting effect can be obtained, giving opportunities for further developments.

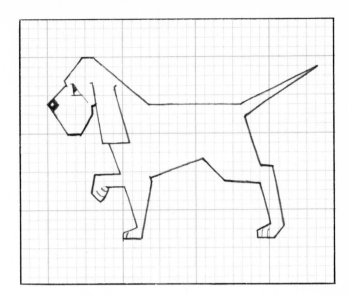

SQUARED PAPER

Graph paper can be bought which has either small or larger squares printed upon it. Keep a few sheets of different kinds in your file ready for use.

You will notice that the squares are all even so that graph paper is very useful if you wish to work out a design on even weave fabric. The lines on the paper will represent the threads in the fabric and the squares represent the spaces between the threads.

Designs such as cross stitch, hardanger and canvas work which are worked over counted thread can all be worked out on graph paper.

In an examination you are sometimes asked to design a fun animal using mainly straight lines. This can easily be done by using graph paper, ruler and pencil. The lines on the paper will help you to be more accurate than you otherwise might be.

A design for a corner is often worked out on graph paper. Draw a line diagonally across the paper from the corner and start drawing from this line which will pass through the centre of your design. Draw one side of the design first and then with the aid of the lines and squares repeat the design on the other side of the line.

Transferring designs to fabrics

PRICK AND POUNCE METHOD

This is a very successful method and the one most widely employed. It can be used on linens, cottons, rayons, silks etc. Proceed as follows.

Take a careful tracing of the design using strong tracing paper. Turn the paper over and place it right side down on a soft pad of folded fabric. Take a needle which is not too thick but long enough to hold comfortably, and perforate the lines of the design by pricking. The pricks should be evenly spaced, fairly close together but not so close that they will run into a large hole. When the pricking is complete hold the paper to the light to see that no part of the tracing has been forgotten.

Lay the paper right side up and rub away the rough edges with sand-paper. Press the fabric which is to be used for the embroidery and pin it out on to a firm board. Lay the tracing right side up on to the fabric and pin it into position.

Make a small pounce pad by rolling a short length of felt and binding it in the middle with thread. The pounce is white powdered chalk or black powdered charcoal. Put a little of the pounce into the lid of a tin

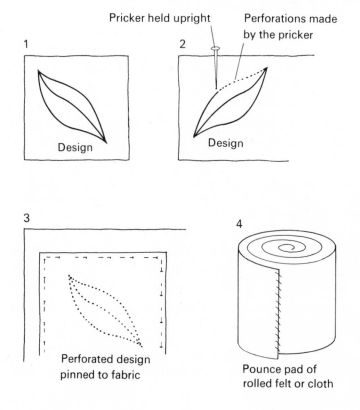

or a saucer, dip the felt pad into it and dab it over the pricked holes of the design. The dabbing needs to be done quite firmly so that the powder will pass through the holes on to the fabric.

After the pouncing remove the tracing paper very carefully and with a fine brush and water colour paint over the design. When the paint is quite dry give the fabric a brisk shake to remove the surplus powder.

TACKING METHOD

Some thick and heavy fabrics as well as felt and piled fabrics will not take the prick and pounce method, so it is best to use the tacking method on these. Lay the traced design on to the fabric and either pin or tack the paper into place. Make small tacking stitches all round the design, sewing through the paper and the fabric. When the tacking is complete tear away the paper; this must be done carefully to avoid pulling the small tacking stitches out of position.

TRANSPARENT FABRICS

Use the fabric itself as the tracing paper by laying it over the design, and trace through using a hard, sharp pencil or rather dry, white paint on a fine brush. Do not use a soft pencil as it tends to smear.

TEMPLATES

A template is a shape made of thin card, board or metal. It is used by being placed on the fabric, held firmly in place, and the shape then being marked round. When a design is being built up templates can be used for marking out repeat shapes either on to the drawing paper or directly on to the fabric. Traditionally templates are used in English quilting and in patchwork (see pages 57 and 59).

NET

The design must be drawn boldly on to firm paper, using special wax blue tracing paper if you can, and the net must be tacked firmly to the paper along all four sides. The outlines of the design are then darned in using a blunt-pointed needle and a fairly thick thread. Keep the thread in as continuous a line as possible; it may be necessary to go over a line twice to keep the continuity and to avoid breaking off a thread. Do not use a knot or fasten off; the new thread should be darned in, slightly overlapping the old. The waxed tracing paper is removed when the outlines are complete and the filling-in stitches are then worked.

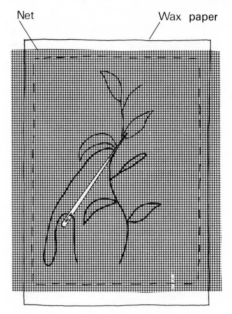

Net .... Wax paper

Enlarging and reducing the design

You may be asked to enlarge or reduce a design, having been given only one of the new measurements required. This is what you do.

Draw a rectangle to enclose the original design. Join two diagonally opposite corners and extend this line beyond the edge of the rectangle.

If the base measurement has been given, draw a line out horizontally, from the corner where the diagonal line protrudes, to the given measurement. From the far end of this line take a line up to meet the diagonal line. Complete the new rectangle to the new size.

If the vertical or height measurement has been given, draw a line upwards from the corner where the diagonal line protrudes, to the given measurement. From the top of the line draw a line at right angles until it meets the diagonal line. Complete the new rectangle.

Having drawn the new rectangle or frame, divide both the original and the new one into small squares of equal size. It will then be possible to reproduce the design to the new dimensions by checking the layout of the original design against the squares on both rectangles.

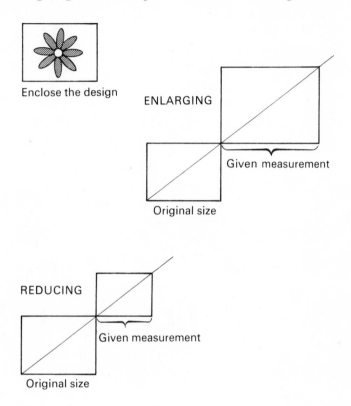

Enclose the design

ENLARGING

Given measurement

Original size

REDUCING

Given measurement

Original size

Collage

A collage is the building up of a picture from bits and pieces of fabric and odds and ends of other materials. If the collage is to be entered for an embroidery examination, the pieces must be stitched to the background wherever possible, although they may be lightly glued to hold them in position first of all.

String collage of an oak leaf. PAT REILLY (14).

It is often difficult to know how to start a collage but one of the easiest ways is to make a string collage.

Draw a leaf or fish shape directly on to the background fabric with tailor's chalk to give the desired outline. Collect as many different textures and thicknesses of string as you possibly can, and fill in the chosen shape with lines of string, following the shape and adding coils and knots wherever a variation of line is required to give interest.

String can also be frayed, and chopped string can be sprinkled on to a lightly glued surface. It is a good idea to spend a little time playing with string and seeing what ideas you can work out for yourself. Stick these ideas on to a piece of card for future reference. For your first collage use Copydex and stick the string to the background. You will soon realise that some string behaves differently to some others and that you cannot always make it do what you have in mind, so that you have to change your ideas as you go along.

This changing of ideas according to the feel of the piece which is being used is what collage is all about. It is an exciting experiment in the use of applied fabrics and a challenge in the use of varied materials and threads. You will begin to understand about texture, about the effect of light on fabrics and embroidery threads, about nap, weaves and control of threads, how a few stitches will add or detract from the design, and how to add richness by using beads etc. or gold or silver kid.

Your first fabric collage could be a follow-on exercise in related shapes, mentioned earlier in the book. Take your chosen paper shape and draw in the varied lines across the space. Cut along the lines within the shape, number and separate the pieces.

Lay the pieces together again on a contrasting sheet of paper and then move them until you are satisfied with the effect created, but remember to keep them in their numbered order.

When you are quite sure of the positions, pin the design pieces of paper down and lay a sheet of tracing paper over the whole. Pin the tracing paper so that it cannot move and draw round the shapes which are showing through, writing the numbers yet again on to the tracing paper. Join each shape to its neighbour with a connecting line either straight or curved, and then lift the tracing paper off. Cut out the numbered shapes. The connecting lines will act as guide lines when applying the shapes to their background fabric.

Choose your background cloth, usually plain fabric, which must be strong enough to support any applied fabrics or objects which you may be going to use. Pin the tracing paper on to the background fabric and with

Shapes numbered and separated

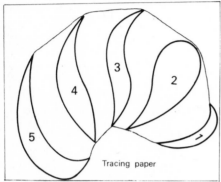

Shapes separated and joined
with a connecting line

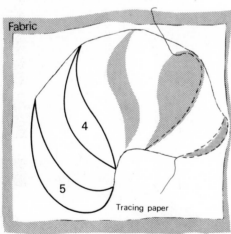

Outline the spaces with
fine running stitches

fine running stitches outline the spaces which now show quite clearly. The tracing paper can then be taken away as you will have marked the positions for your shapes.

Some of the outlined spaces can be embroidered, others can be appliquéd; you will think of your own ideas. The numbered shapes can now be used as templates for the pieces which are going to be applied.

If you are going to appliqué the pieces to the background it is a good plan to pin them into position and then stand well back and look at the effect. You will have chosen the fabrics etc. by looking down at them, but when they are in position on the backcloth and are placed in a hanging position you may well find that your ideas have to change because of the effect of light on the textures of the fabrics. At several stages of the work it is as well to stand back and take a long look, even leaving the work overnight if you feel that something is not working out as you expected. Often an idea will come when you look unexpectedly at the work again.

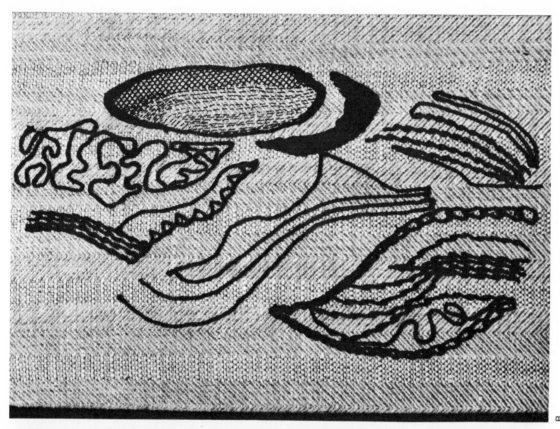

B

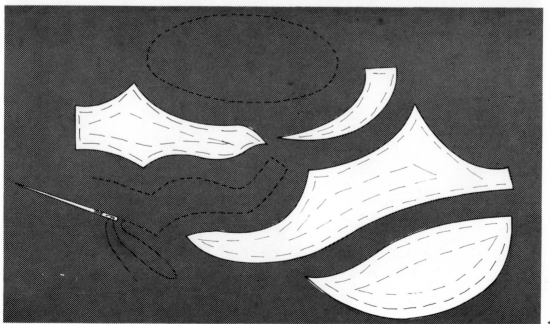

A

25

Equipment

The embroidress should have the following as the basic equipment for her work: needles, threads, scissors, tambour frame, black and white pounce, tailor's chalk, tape measure, thimble, pins, an iron and an ironing board. For designing you will need a drawing board, drawing pins, a variety of card and paper, including tissue and graph, compass, ruler, set square, protractor. A stilleto is useful for making holes and a pot of glue such as Copydex may also be necessary. Templates (either purchased or self-made) are also needed.

Needles

The needles most commonly used in embroidery are:
SHARP A general purpose needle. Size 8 is the most popular.
BETWEEN A short needle, sometimes easier to handle than a sharp.
DARNER A long needle with a large eye; mixed sizes thick and thin.
CREWEL An embroidery needle with a large eye.
TAPESTRY A needle with a blunt point and a long eye, for use mainly on canvas embroidery or for counted thread work. A tapestry needle is made in sizes from 13 to 26 and all other needles are in sizes from 1 to 12. The higher the number, the finer the needle; the lower the number, the larger the eye.

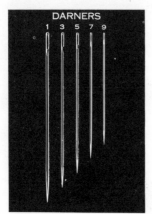

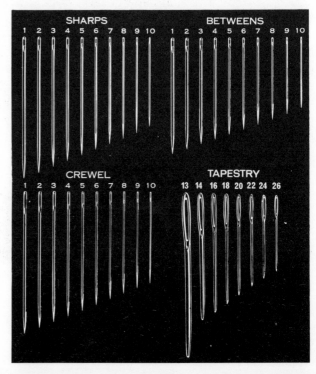

1

2

3

4

5

6

7

8 & 9

Some examples of the many embroidery threads available.

Threads

All of the following threads are easily obtainable from most haberdashery counters in big stores and from specialist shops selling needlecraft equipment:

METALLIC THREADS	TAPISSERIE WOOL
STRANDED COTTON	PLASTRAW
COTON A BRODER	RAYON CROCHET YARN
SOFT EMBROIDERY	LUREX THREADS
CREWEL WOOL	

A wide variety of wools can also be purchased. Interesting threads can also be obtained by unravelling woven fabric; these are particularly useful when doing a collage as the twist in the fibre gives a pleasing effect.

Fabrics

There is a wide variety of fabrics for you to choose from and learning to choose does indeed call for a lot of patience. Only when you have got the feel of the needle going through the fabric and seen the thread lying on it will you be able to tell what thickness of thread and what size of needle is required for the particular fabric and whether it will serve what you had in mind for your particular piece of work.

When choosing a fabric many things must be borne in mind: will it need to be washed? Is it thick enough or too fine for the piece of work you are going to do? Is the colour right? Is the texture correct? How will the texture affect the design? If the finished piece of work is to be hung then you must hold the fabric up before buying to see the effect of the light on the texture. It sometimes alters considerably under these conditions.

If you can afford to do so, buy a small piece of the fabric and experiment with it first; it may have a definite grain so that the stitches look better worked across the grain than with it. Try the simple running, back and loop stitches and this will give you an idea of the size of needle to use and the thickness of thread and how the two marry together.

Remnants of all kinds of fabric should be saved and stored. Dress-making and soft furnishing pieces should be sorted into colours before storing. Printed fabrics should always be used with discretion as their ready-made design could dominate or distort what you are trying to build up. But often the discreet, and sometimes the bold, designs of furnishing fabrics lend themselves very well to emphasis by embroidery, when made into a wall panel for example.

String bags in which carrots are delivered to the shops, when washed and softened make excellent leaves in a piece of collage. Net tights, plastic lemon bags, fine leather gloves, pieces of hessian, velvet ribbons etc. are all useful items to store.

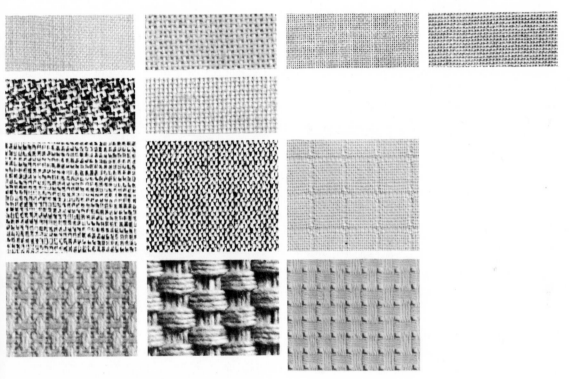

Some of the wide range of fabrics designed especially for embroidery. Top row: four embroidery linens; second row (L to R): Granite and linen scrim; third row: cotton scrim, linen union background fabric and Cordova; fourth row: Java, Malleeta and medium cross stitch canvas.

29

Frames

There are two types of frames in general use: the round wooden frame called a tambour frame, and the square frame. The former is used for small pieces of work and the latter for much larger pieces. Setting the fabric into the frame is known as 'dressing' the frame.

A TAMBOUR FRAME is composed of two circles of wood which fit one into the other and are held tight with a screw on the outer ring.

To prepare the frame, separate the rings and bind the inner ring with soft fabric wound round and round it. This will prevent the wood from marking the fabric. Lay the fabric over the inner ring and place the outer ring over it, tightening the screw to hold the fabric firmly. Pull it gently into place so that the grain of the fabric is running true and is not distorted. If it is not straight, loosen the screw slightly and gently pull the fabric before tightening it again.

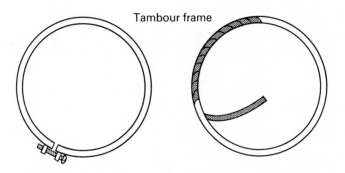

Tambour frame

A SQUARE FRAME consists of four pieces, together with four wooden pegs or split pins. The two rollers, with holes at either end, have a strip of webbing tacked firmly down their length. The stretchers are flat laths with a line of holes bored in them. These stretchers fit through the holes at the end of the rollers.

When putting on the fabric, the grain should run from roller to roller and the selvedge sides should face the stretchers.

Mark the centre points of the fabric and of the webbing. Place the centre points together, fabric to webbing. Oversew the two together starting from the centre points and working outwards. Sew a length of strong tape to each of the 'selvedge' edges.

The stretchers are now inserted into the holes at the end of the rollers, and the rollers are pegged as far apart as they will stretch. The placing of the pegs must be the same on each side. Take a strong thread, attach

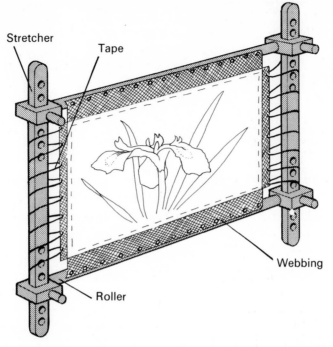

Stretcher
Tape
Webbing
Roller

it to the top of each lath and lace it through the taped edge and over the stretchers, working down the frame and tying off the thread to the bottom of the lath in such a way that it could be released if the work should need tightening.

MAKE YOUR OWN FRAME

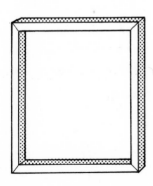

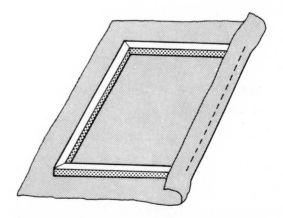

1 Either use an old picture frame or join together four strips of wood.

2 Lay the frame on the fabric. Bring the edge of the fabric over the frame and staple or tack down.

31

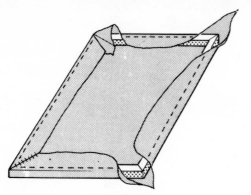

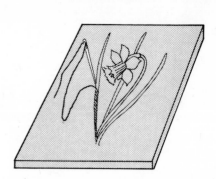

3 Mitre the corners for a neat fit.

4 Use the frame by passing the needle downwards and upwards through the fabric.

TO MITRE A CORNER

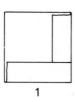

1

Make and press a single turning along both sides.

2

Open the turnings so that crease lines are visible.

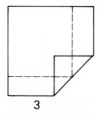

3

Fold the corner diagonally laying one crease line over the other.

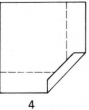

4

Trim away the material leaving a narrow turning.

5

Fold back the turning and oversew the fold.

Stitches 1

Outline stitches

STEM STITCH

Point the needle towards yourself. Work away from yourself. Take regular stitches along the line of the design. The stitches may be either slightly slanting or straight along the line. Keep the working thread to the right of the line.

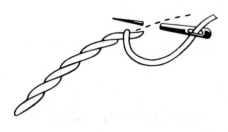

RUNNING STITCH

Start with a double back stitch. Work from right to left and make three or four stitches at the same time. The stitches and spaces should be of equal length or the under stitch could be half the size of the upper stitch.

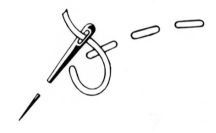

BACK STITCH

Work from right to left. Bring the needle through, then take a small backward stitch through the fabric and bring the needle through again a little in front of the previous stitch. Take the needle back each time to the end of the last stitch.

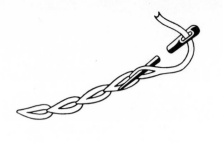

SPLIT STITCH
This is worked the same as for stem stitch except that the needle pierces the working thread as seen in the diagram.

SCROLL STITCH
Work from left to right. Bring the needle through to the right side, loop the thread into a circle from right to left, take a small slanting stitch to the left inside the loop, keep the thread under the point of the needle. Pull the needle through and repeat.

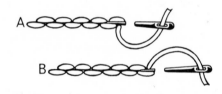

CABLE STITCH
Work from left to right. Bring the needle through on the line of the design, insert the needle to the right on the line and bring it out half-way along the length of the stitch, with the thread below the needle (A). Work the next stitch in the same way but with the thread above the needle (B). Keep the thread alternating below and above the needle.

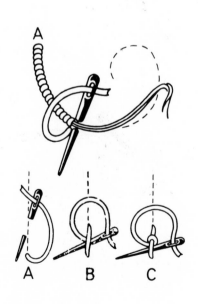

OVERCAST OR TRAILING STITCH
Bring the laid threads through at (A) and hold with the left thumb. Bring the working thread through also at (A). Work small satin stitches closely together over the laid threads. To finish take the end of the laid threads through to the back.

PORTUGUESE STEM STITCH
Begin as for simple stem stitch (A). Pull the thread through and pass the needle under the stitch just made but *not* through the fabric (B). Pass the needle

under the same stitch below the first coil (C). Make another stem stitch (D). Pass the needle twice under the stitch just made and under the previous stitch (E). Stitches will be formed as in (F).

Chained stitches

CHAIN STITCH

Work towards yourself. Bring the thread out at the top of the design line and hold the thread down with your left thumb. Insert the needle where it last emerged and bring the point out a short distance away. Pull the thread through, keeping the working thread under the needle, and holding the thread down with your thumb until the stitch is made.

DAISY STITCH OR DETACHED CHAIN

Work in the same way as for chain stitch (A) but secure each loop at the foot with a small stitch (B).

TWISTED CHAIN STITCH

Start as for simple chain stitch, but insert the needle close to the last loop and take a small slanting stitch, coming out on the line of the design. The loops of this stitch must be worked close together to get a good effect.

OPEN CHAIN STITCH

This stitch may be used for filling in shapes of varying width. Bring the needle through at (A), hold the thread down with the thumb, and insert the needle at (B). Bring the needle through at (C) at the required depth of the

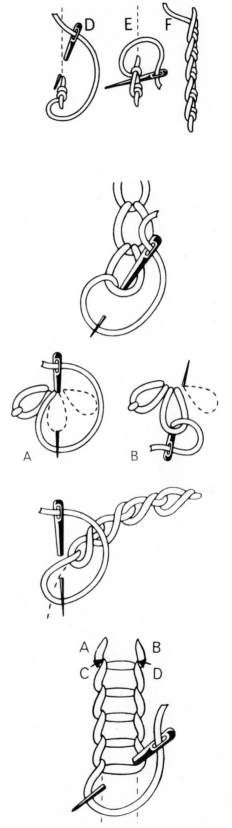

35

stitch. Leave the loop slightly loose and insert the needle at (D), bring it through keeping the thread under the point of the needle. To finish secure the last loop with a small stitch at each side.

ROSETTE CHAIN STITCH

Work this stitch across two parallel lines. Bring the thread through at the right hand end of the upper line, pass the thread across to the left side and hold down with the left thumb. Insert the needle into the upper line a short distance from where the thread emerged and bring it out just above the lower line, passing the thread under the needle point (A). Pull the needle through and pass the needle under the top thread (B) without picking up any of the fabric.

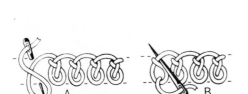

WHEAT-EAR STITCH

Work two straight stitches at (A) and (B). Bring the needle through at (C) and then pass the needle under the two straight stitches without entering the fabric. Insert the needle at (C) and make the next two straight stitches (D) and (E).

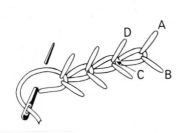

CABLE STITCH

Bring the needle through at (A) and hold the thread down with the left thumb. Pass the needle from right to left under the working thread, then twist the needle back over the working thread to the right, still keeping the thread under the thumb. Take a stitch of the required length and pull the thread through.

Flat stitches

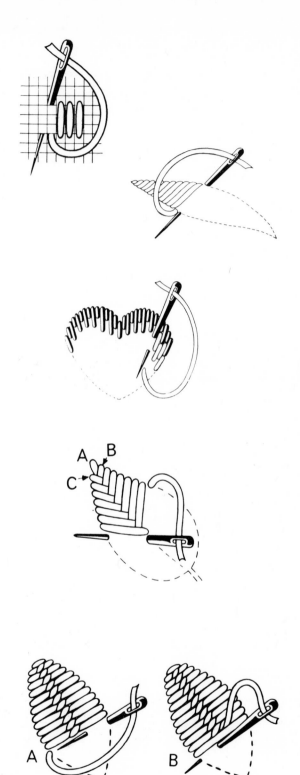

SATIN STITCH

These are straight stitches worked closely together across the shape. To give a raised effect running stitches or chain stitches may be worked first and the straight stitches sewn over these. It is better not to have the stitches too long, and care must be taken to keep the edges neat. This stitch is also used in counted thread embroidery.

LONG AND SHORT STITCH

This form of satin stitch is so called because in the first row the stitches are of different lengths. Afterwards they are of regular lengths away from the first stitches, keeping the uneven appearance.

FISHBONE STITCH

Bring the needle through the fabric at (A) and make a small straight stitch along the centre of the shape. Bring the thread through again at (B) and make a sloping stitch across the central line at the base of the first stitch. Bring the needle through at (C) and make a similar sloping stitch to overlap the previous stitch. Continue working alternately on each side until the shape is filled.

ROUMANIAN STITCH

Bring the thread through at the top left of the shape, and take a stitch on the right side of the shape keeping the thread below the needle. Take a stitch at the left side of the shape with the thread above the needle. Keep the stitches close together for a good effect.

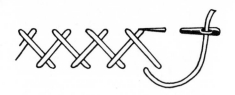

HERRINGBONE STITCH

Work from left to right. Bring the needle through on the lower line at the left side and insert on the upper line a little to the right taking a small stitch to the left with the thread below the needle. Insert the needle on the lower line a little to the right and take a small stitch to the left with the thread above the needle. The best effect is obtained by keeping the spaces between the stitches of equal size.

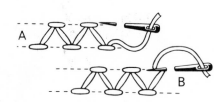

CHEVRON STITCH

Work from left to right. Bring the needle through on the lower line at the left side, insert the needle a little to the right on the same line and take a small stitch to the left coming out half-way along the stitch being made. Insert the needle on the upper line a little to the right and take a small stitch to the left (A). Insert the needle again on the same line a little to the right and take a small stitch to the left coming out at the centre (B). Work alternately on the upper and lower lines.

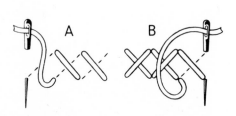

CROSS STITCH

Bring the needle through on the lower line and insert the needle in the upper line a little to the left. Bring the needle out on the lower line immediately below the point of entry on the upper line. Continue making this stitch to the end of the row. Complete the other half of the cross on the return journey. On the right side of the work all the top stitches should lie in one direction, on the wrong side of the work the stitches will be vertical parallel lines.

SEEDING–A FILLING STITCH

This is a small straight stitch of even length placed at random over the surface to be embroidered.

Looped stitches

BLANKET STITCH

Work from left to right. Bring the needle out on the lower edge, insert the needle in the upper line and make a straight downward stitch with the thread under the needle point. Pull up the thread to form a loop.

CLOSED BLANKET STITCH

These stitches are made in pairs to form triangles. Bring the needle through at (A), insert the needle at (B), and with the thread under the needle bring it through at (C). Insert the needle again at (B) and bring it through at (D). Repeat.

FEATHER STITCH

Bring the needle through to the right side of the fabric, and hold the thread down with the left thumb. Insert the needle a little to the right on the same level and take a small stitch down to the centre, keeping the thread under the point of the needle. Insert the needle a little to the left on the same level and take a stitch down to the centre as before, keeping the thread under the point of the needle. Work the stitches alternately from side to side.

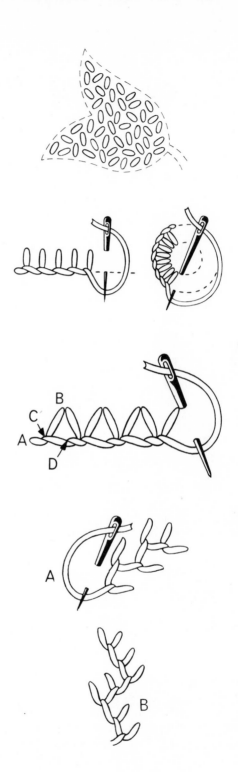

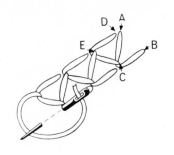

CLOSED FEATHER STITCH

This stitch is worked along two parallel lines. Bring the needle through at (A) and with the thread under the needle, take a stitch from (B) to (C). Pass the thread over to the left and with the thread under the needle take a stitch from (D) to (E). Repeat these two stitches.

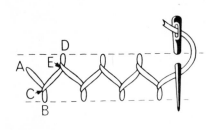

OPEN CRETAN STITCH

Bring the needle through at (A) and with the thread above the needle insert the needle at (B) and bring it out at (C). With the thread below the needle, insert the needle at (D) and bring it out at (E). All stitches lie at right angles to the guiding lines and are spaced at regular intervals.

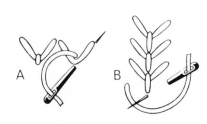

FLY STITCH

Bring the needle through to the right side of the fabric and hold the thread down with the left thumb. Insert the needle to the right on the same level and take a small stitch downwards to the centre with the thread below the needle. Pull the needle through and insert again below the stitch at the centre, bringing it through into position for the next stitch. The holding-down stitch may be short or long, and the stitch may be worked singly or in horizontal rows (A) or vertically (B).

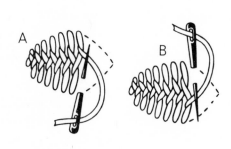

CRETAN STITCH

Bring the needle through at the left hand side and take a small stitch with the needle pointing upwards and with the thread under the needle point (A).

Take a stitch on the opposite side with the needle pointing downwards and the thread under the needle point (B).

VANDYKE STITCH
Bring the thread through at (A). Take a small horizontal stitch at (B) and insert the needle at (C). Bring the thread through at (D). Without going into the fabric pass the needle under the crossed threads at (B) and insert the needle at (E). Be careful not to pull the stitches too tightly, otherwise the evenness of the plait through the centre will be lost.

TO MAKE A SPIDER'S WEB
1 Sew a fly stitch.

2 Bring the needle back to the centre and add another stitch of equal length (A). Repeat once more (B).

3 You will have an odd number of stitches. Bring the needle up to the centre and weave the thread over and under these stitches until the web is complete.

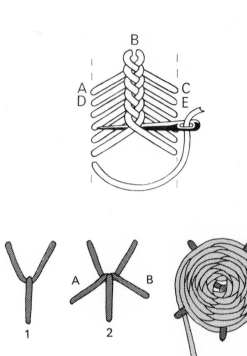

Knotted stitches

FRENCH KNOTS
Bring the needle out at the required position, hold the thread down with the left thumb, and wind the thread two or three times round the needle (A). Hold the thread firmly, twist the needle back to the starting point and insert it close to where the thread first came through. Pull the needle through to the back of the fabric and fasten off for a single knot, or bring the needle through again for the next stitch.

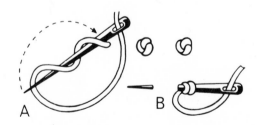

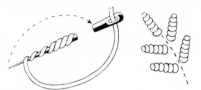

BULLION STITCH

This is a decorative back stitch. Use a needle with a small eye, as it will pass more easily through the coils. Pick up a piece of fabric on the needle the required length of the stitch. Leave the needle in the work and twist the thread round the needle point as many times as would be required to equal the *length* of the *back stitch*. Hold the left thumb on the coiled thread and pull the needle through; without moving the thumb, turn the needle back to where it was inserted and insert in the same place. Pull the thread through until the bullion stitch lies flat.

CORAL STITCH

Bring the needle through at the right end of the design line, lay the thread along the design line and hold it down with the left thumb. Take a small stitch under the line and the thread, and pull through bringing the needle over the lower thread as in the diagram.

KNOTTED CABLE CHAIN STITCH

Work from right to left. Bring the needle through at (A) and place the thread along the design line. Pass the thread under the needle and take a stitch at (B). (This is a *Coral knot*.) Pass the needle under the stitch between (A) and (B) without piercing the fabric (C). With the thread under the needle take a slanting stitch across the line at (D), close to the coral knot. Pull the thread through to form a chain stitch.

Stitches 2

Couching

SIMPLE COUCHING

Lay a thread along the line of the design, and with another thread catch it down to the fabric with a small stitch.

ROUMANIAN COUCHING

Bring the needle through on the left and carry the thread across the space to be filled. Take a small stitch on the right with the thread above the needle (A). Take small stitches along the line at regular intervals (B and C), to the end of the laid thread. Bring the needle through in position for the next laid line (D).

BOKHARA COUCHING

Work in the same way as Roumanian stitch but make the small stitches at regular intervals to form pattern lines across the shape. Pull the stitches tight, but leave the laid threads slightly loose.

JACOBEAN COUCHING

OR TRELLIS

Make long, evenly spaced stitches across the space horizontally and then vertically. Where the laid threads cross make a small slanting stitch or cross stitch to hold them down to the fabric.

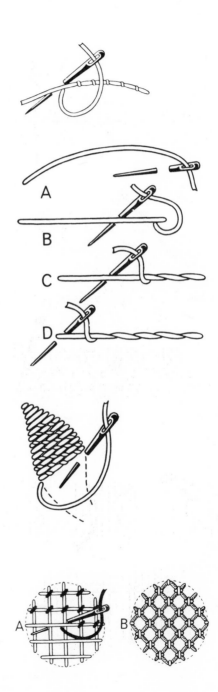

Composite stitches

These stitches are made by sewing the first stitches into the fabric and then passing another thread through the stitches but not into the fabric.

PEKINESE STITCH
Work a row of back stitch then interlace another thread in a forward and backward movement to form a loop. The loops should be pulled slightly to lie flat on the fabric.

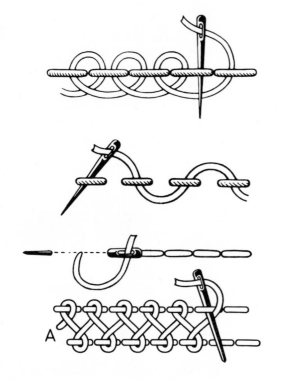

LACED RUNNING STITCH
Work a row of running stitches and lace with a contrasting colour thread. The lacing thread is not sewn to the fabric.

INTERLACED BAND
Make two rows of back stitching with the stitches on the lower line coming opposite the ends of the stitches on the top line. Start from the left, pass another thread over and under the lines of backstitching.

Drawn fabric or Counted thread stitches

FOUR-SIDED STITCH
Bring the thread through to the right side. Insert the needle at (A) four threads up, bring the needle through at (B) four threads down and four threads to the left. Insert the needle at the bottom of the first stitch, and bring it out at (C) four threads up and four threads to the left. Insert the needle again at (A) and bring it out at (B). The work is turned round to work the return row.

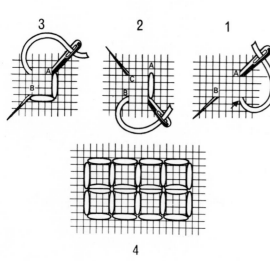

44

WAVE STITCH FILLING

Work from right to left. Bring the needle to the right side. Insert the needle at (A) four threads up and two threads to the right, bring it through at (B) four threads to the left. Insert the needle at the bottom of the first stitch and bring it through at (C) four threads to the left. Continue to the end of the row, and turn the fabric round for working the second row. Work into the holes of the previous stitches to form a diamond pattern.

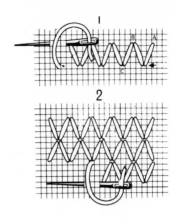

MOSAIC FILLING

Work four blocks of satin stitch to form a square, with an equal number of stitches in each block and worked over an equal number of threads. Bring the thread through to the right hand corner of the inner square and work a four sided stitch. Finish with a cross stitch in the centre.

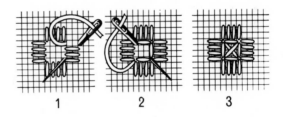

HOLBEIN
OR DOUBLE RUNNING STITCH

Work from right to left. Make a row of running stitches over and under three threads of fabric, changing direction to make a design. On the return journey work in the same way from left to right, filling in the spaces left by the first row.

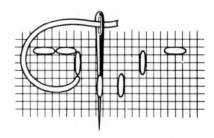

DIAGONAL RAISED BAND

Work diagonally from lower right to top left corner. Bring the needle through to the right side, insert it four threads up (A) and bring it out two threads down and two threads to the left (B). Continue to the end of the row. To return insert the needle at (C) and bring it through at (D). Pull all the stitches firmly.

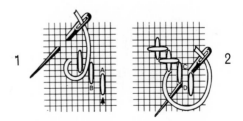

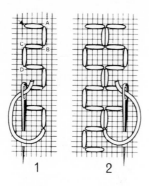

1   2

HONEYCOMB FILLING

Work from the top downwards. Bring the needle through to the right side. Insert it at (A) four threads to the right, bring it through at (B) four threads down. Insert again at (A) and bring it through at (B), insert at (C) four threads to the left, bring the needle through at (D). Continue in this way for the length required. Turn the fabric round to work the next and any following rows. Pull all stitches firmly.

Drawn thread stitches

The important difference between drawn thread work and drawn fabric work is this. In drawn thread work the bands of thread are withdrawn (pulled out) before the stitching is started. In drawn fabric work the threads are drawn (pulled) together with the sewing thread to form the patterns.

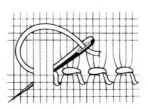

HEMSTITCH

Cut the threads at the centre of one side of the fabric and withdraw the threads to the required depth. Leave the shortened threads loose for darning in. Bring the needle through to the right side of the fabric, pass it behind four loose threads, and bring it out two threads down in the fabric, ready for the next stitch.

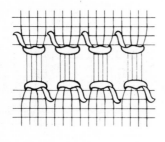

LADDER HEMSTITCH

Work as for hemstitch, sewing first one edge and then the other.

ZIG-ZAG HEMSTITCH

Work as for hemstitch but make sure that there are an even number of threads grouped together. Work the second row by grouping together half the threads from one group and half from the adjacent group.

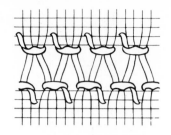

DOUBLE OR ITALIAN HEMSTITCH

Withdraw the threads from the fabric for the required depth, miss the same number of threads and withdraw another band to equal the first. Bring the needle out four threads to the left in the top band of threads, pass the needle behind the four threads, bring it out where the thread first emerged (A). Pass the needle down over the fabric and under four threads in the lower band. Pass the needle over the same four threads and under the fabric; bring it out four threads to the left, in the top band.

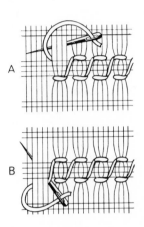

INTERLACED HEMSTITCH

Withdraw a wide band of threads and work ladder hemstitch. Pass the working thread across the front of two groups of threads and insert the needle from left to right under the second group (A). Twist the second group over the first group by inserting the needle under the first group from right to left (B). Pull the thread through. The interlaced thread should be pulled firm enough to lie in position through the centre of the twisted groups.

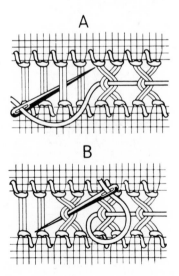

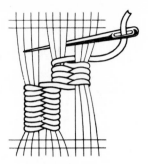

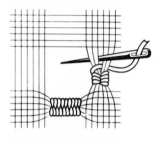

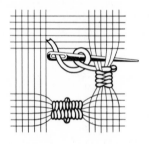

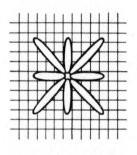

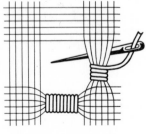

Hardanger stitches

NEEDLEWEAVING
Withdraw a number of threads to the depth required. Work blocks of weaving to fill the space. The blocks are worked across the loose threads by weaving another thread over and under the number of threads you have decided upon for the pattern.

WOVEN BARS
Withdraw threads in bands on the fabric. Weave over and under an even number of threads to the end of the space. The woven bars may run either horizontally or vertically.

WOVEN BARS WITH SIMPLE PICOT
Work as for woven bars but half-way along the woven bar twist the thread once round the needle, insert the needle for weaving and repeat on the next stitch to make a picot on each side of the bar.

STAR EYELET
All the stitches are worked from the same central hole. There should be eight stitches worked over an eight thread square.

OVERCAST BARS
Withdraw the required number of threads and form the bars by overcasting until the group of threads is completely covered.

nsertion stitches

These stitches are used for joining two pieces of fabric together by a decorative method.

KNOTTED INSERTION
Make a small blanket stitch into the edge of the fabric and make a second stitch over the loop as shown in the diagram. The stitches are made alternately on each piece of fabric to be joined. A piece of paper may be tacked behind the two edges of fabric to keep them evenly apart, before the insertion stitches are made.

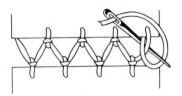

TWISTED INSERTION
A small stitch is taken alternately on each piece of the fabric to be joined. The needle must enter the fabric from beneath and must be twisted once round the thread before entering the fabric for the opposite stitch.

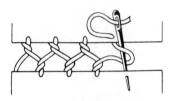

Mathematical embroidery

Mathematical embroidery, or Curve stitchery as it is sometimes called, is a very old method of expression work in mathematics. The simplest patterns are obtained by joining holes which are equally spaced on straight lines or circles.

In the case of two straight lines the resulting envelope is the parabola. More complicated curves result from the use of circles, where the stitches bounce off the circumference at right angles.

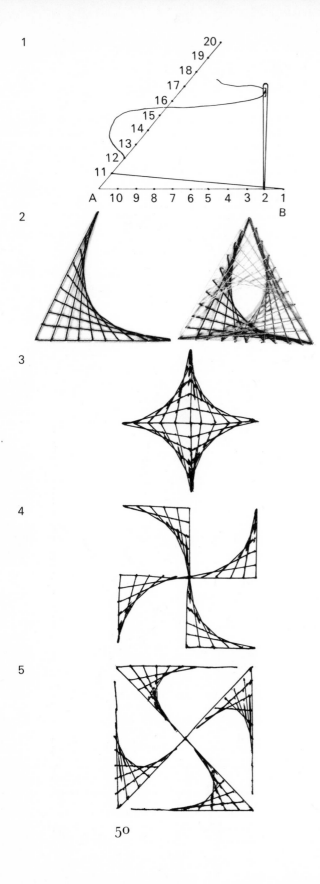

The most impressive effect is obtained by stitching in white thread on black cloth or vice versa.

Diagram 1 shows how to stitch a parabola. Take a piece of thin paper and draw an angle with two arms of equal length. Divide each arm along its length with equally spaced marks. Number as shown. Cut away the paper inside the angle and pin the rest to the fabric as a guide. Bring the needle up through the fabric at point 1 and down at 11, then up at 12 and down at 2 and so on.

Diagram 2 shows parabola curves worked on each angle of an equilateral triangle.

Diagram 3 shows a parabola stitched at the inside angles of a square which has been divided into four equal parts with a horizontal and a vertical line.

Diagram 4 shows a parabola stitched at the outside edge of a square which has been divided in the same way as 3.

Diagram 5 shows a parabola stitched at the angles obtained by dividing a square diagonally in both directions.

Diagram 6 (p. 51) shows parabola curves worked across alternate segments of a circle which has been divided into six equal parts.

Experiment with straight lines and circles. It is possible to make animal and bird designs, etc. using this technique.

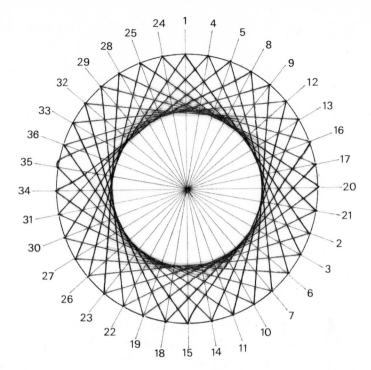

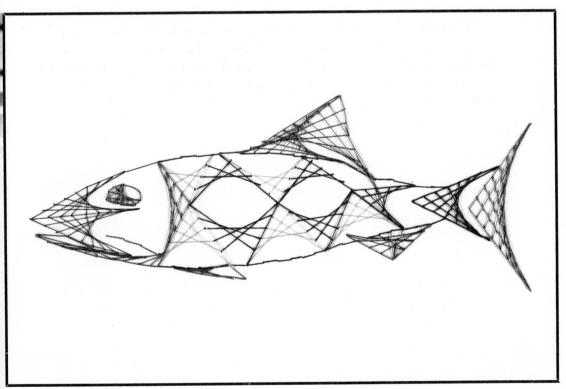

Other sewing techniques

Padding

The object of padding is to create a raised surface which will give height and added interest to a piece of embroidery. The added interest often comes from the shadows cast from the padded piece when the finished embroidery is hanging. Height and shadow can also be obtained by adding objects which are not padded.

A piece of foam is a good medium for a first experiment. Cut the foam to the required shape and trim away the edges by slanting, to soften the effect. Cut a piece of fabric at least 2·5 cm larger than the foam and run a gathering thread round the outside, about 6 mm away from the edge. Put the foam inside the fabric and pull up the gathering thread until the fabric is smooth on the outside of the shape. Fasten off the thread. Stick the shape to the background with a small dab of adhesive in the centre and from the back of the work sew a few stitches round the edge to hold the shape in position.

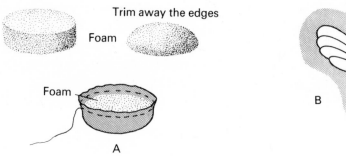

Trim away the edges

Foam

Foam

A

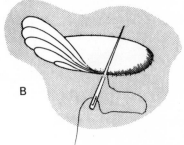

B

Layers of felt are often used for padding. Cut several layers of the shape required, making each piece slightly smaller than the last. Stick the smallest piece down first, followed by the others and keeping all the centres carefully over each other. If the padding is to be covered with fabric do this next, turning the edges under the top piece as you sew it down. If you are going to embroider over the felt padding handsew the felt to the background making the stitches as inconspicuous as possible.

Take a piece of fabric of the shape required and with a turning of 2·5 cm and put in the gathering thread as before. Use cotton wool or terylene fibre and push it into the shape until the shape is firm and without wrinkles in the fabric. Apply to the background by sticking and sewing.

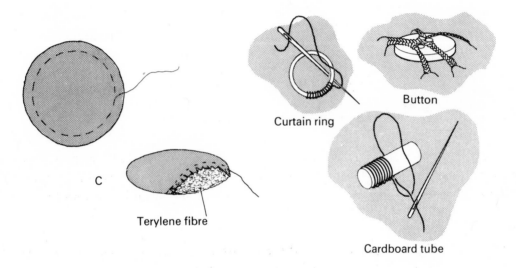

Curtain ring

Button

c

Terylene fibre

Cardboard tube

Solid objects can be used for padding. Take a button and sew it to the background. Make large stitches across the button from the centre outwards and needleweave into the threads for a textured effect. Curtain rings sewn down with blanket stitch give a raised effect. Cardboard tubes (sweet tubes) can be covered with fabric or held down with stitches passing over the tube and into the background fabric.

You may be able to think of other ways of obtaining padded or raised effects.

Appliqué

Appliqué is the fastening down of one piece of fabric to another. There are various ways of doing this and it is a useful exercise to experiment with all of the methods to learn the different techniques involved and to know how fabrics and stitches behave under different circumstances.

Cut out a variety of shapes using a wide range of fabrics of differing textures. The shape should be tacked to the background to hold it in place with the true grain of both fabrics in the same direction. Then try the following methods of fastening down.

Use flat embroidery stitches such as herringbone, chain stitch and blanket stitch to hold the edges down.

Cover the edges completely with long and short stitches using a thicker thread. The edge of the shape will then become important.

Couch a bouclé or similar thread down to the outline of the shape, giving an impression of texture.

Fray the edges of the piece and sew down with small straight stitches using matching thread. The stitches will hardly show.

Machine stitching—across the shape, zig-zag stitch over the edge or at random over the shape.

Each of these methods will give an interesting way of holding down one piece of fabric to another.

For soft fabrics turn the edge under before applying to the background cloth. If the applied piece has straight edges, mitre the corners; if the edges are curved inwards, small snips must be made before the turning will lie flat. If the edge is curved outward it must be clipped before the turning is made. If the fabric is suitable the turning can be pressed down with a hot iron and then tacked directly on to the background fabric; if not the turning should be tacked before applying.

Rug wool, string of different textures, ribbons, pieces of bamboo, orange sticks, wire, etc. are just a few things which could be appliquéd to the fabric by means of stitches.

An example of appliqué work in the Victoria and Albert Museum. (Crown copyright.)

Quilting

ENGLISH QUILTING

In traditional English quilting the designs are transferred to the fabric by the use of templates. The overall design is usually drawn out on paper beforehand so that the quilter knows exactly where to place the design on the fabric. When the work is framed and tacked ready for quilting, the first template is laid in place and it is then scratched round with a needle point. This marks the fabric well enough for the stitching to be worked. It is usual to work each shape before scratching and working the next one. Furnishing fabric with interesting designs can also be used and the design already on the fabric stitched round to form the quilting.

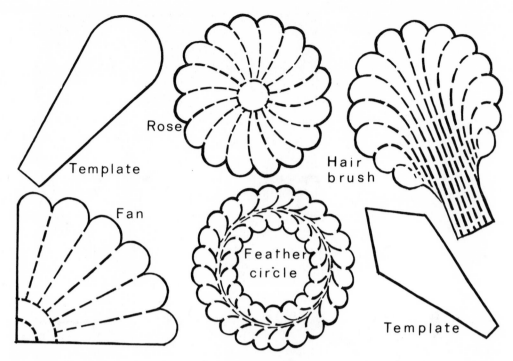

Templates for quilting.

Three layers are used in English quilting. The top layer is often of silk or satin, the inner layer is of wadding or terylene filling, and the under layer is of soft fabric. It is an advantage to warm the wadding first to allow it to fluff up; the needle will then penetrate more easily.

The three layers are tacked together starting from the centre and working outwards. Tack vertically and horizontally, but do not pull the tacking stitches tight. Take the first template, lay it in position and scratch round the shape with the needle point. Small running stitches are used to sew straight lines and stab stitch is used for sewing round curves. Stab stitch is worked one stitch at a time, pushing the needle through to the back of the work, then bringing it right up to the front of the work and so on.

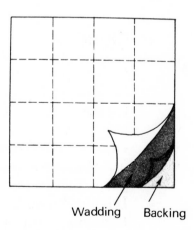

Wadding   Backing

ITALIAN QUILTING

For Italian quilting two layers of fabric are needed. The design is stitched through the upper and backing fabrics and the padding wool is inserted between the two layers afterwards.

The top layer is usually silk, semi-transparent silk, or organdie. The under layer must be of loosely woven fabric such as butter muslin. The padding is a special soft kind of cotton known as quilting wool. It can be bought in brilliant colours which give a glowing effect when the top layer is of transparent fabric.

The design is always formed of two parallel rows. Transfer designs can be bought from the shops or you can make your own by drawing parallel lines to the shape you require. The design is always placed on the backing fabric. Tack the two layers together starting from the centre and making sure that no tacking goes into the parallel lines of the design.

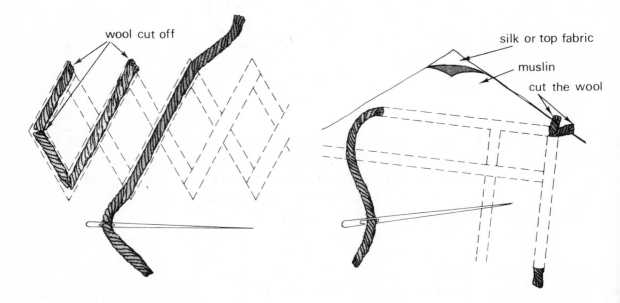

Working from the wrong side because this is where the design can be seen, make small running stitches along the lines of the design. Thread a blunt-ended, large-eyed tapestry needle with several strands of the padding wool.

Starting at one end of the design, pass the needle into the backing fabric and push it along until it comes to the end of a run in the design. Bring the needle through to the top of the backing fabric and cut off the wool. Repeat this through all the lines.

58

When a corner is reached always bring the needle out, cut the wool, insert the needle again in the new direction and go as far as the next corner or stopping point.

Leave the wool lying loosely in the design to obtain a good effect, but have sufficient wool in the needle to fill out the parallel lines.

Patchwork

Throughout history there is evidence that pieces of fabric have been applied for decoration or joined together to make larger pieces of material. Patchwork quilts are possibly the most well-known articles made in this craft. Often the patches are joined together to form a flower or animal shape. When extra padding is inserted under these designs to make them stand out, they are known as raised patches.

The fabric for patches needs to be chosen with some care. It is better not to mix types of fabrics, that is, do not mix silk with cotton, but make all the patches in the same type of fabric. Avoid using man-made fabrics as they fray easily. Lovely silk patches can be made cheaply from men's ties bought perhaps at jumble sales.

Patches are sewn together with small straight stitches, called top sewing. Unlike hemming, the stitches must not slant or they will show on the right side of the work. When making up a pincushion in patchwork the stitching must not only be straight, it must also be close together to prevent the filling from falling out.

The master patterns from which the paper shapes are drawn are called templates. All templates for patchwork are true geometric shapes—they can be hexagon, pentagon, octagon, diamond, triangle and long diamond. Variations of these shapes include church window, the box, coffin, and the shell or clam.

Cut enough firm paper shapes to complete the piece of work before commencing to cover the patches. Check all the paper shapes for size, discarding any which are not accurate. Having chosen the shape which is to be used, make a window. This is made in stiff card as follows. Draw the shape which is to be used. Outside this shape draw another line about 9 mm away. You now have two shapes on the card. Using sharp scissors cut away the inside shape. Cut round the outside shape. The window can now be used as a pattern for cutting the fabric with the turning already allowed for. It is also useful for checking that a particular design on the selected fabric will come accurately within the shape.

Needles: use sharps size 9 or 10
Cotton: use 80 or 100

PREPARATION

Lay the paper shape on to the piece of fabric (patch) and fold over and tack the turning along one side taking the stitches through the paper. When you reach the corner fold a small pleat and tack along the next side. Each time you come to a corner you must fold the pleat in the same direction. Prepare several patches.

Lay two patches together and top sew two edges together, add another patch and continue in this way until the work is complete. Check the work on the right side to see that all the patches are securely fastened together without any gaps. Remove all the tacking stitches and take out the paper shapes. For backing a quilt use sheeting which can be purchased in many colours.

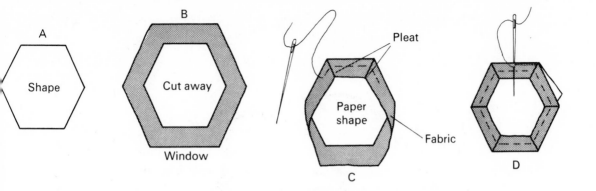

A Shape

B Cut away / Window

C Pleat / Paper shape / Fabric

D

The use of the sewing machine

Modern zig-zag sewing machines have made possible the art of incorporating machine stitches into embroideries. In appliqué, for instance, the machine can be used to hold down the pieces to be applied before hand embroidery is started, or to zig-zag over the edge of the piece for a decorative effect.

Free stitchery can also be used to fill in an outline, or to stand alone as a complete design.

It is necessary to experiment for some little while until you have the feel for this type of embroidery.

Machine embroidery thread is obtainable in thicknesses of 30, 50, 60, 80, and 100; the higher the number, the finer the thread. 50 is the average thickness with which to work and should be used for first attempts. However, if you are working on thick fabric you may find it is better to use a 40 or 50 Sylko.

It would be impossible to describe all the variations possible in machine embroidery in this one chapter, so only the technique for commencing will be given and further books must be studied as your ability improves.

It is essential for the fabric to be kept tight. If you are not able to do this with your hands then an embroidery hoop should be used.

METHOD
Remove the normal presser foot on the machine and replace it with the darning foot. If no darning foot is available the work can still proceed, but the darning foot helps to hold down thin fabric.

Lower the feed (dog) teeth so that the stitches can go in any direction. The machine manufacturer's book will show you how to do this.

Victoria and Albert Museum. Crown copyright.

62

Stretch the fabric into the embroidery hoop, and place the hoop under the needle, with the fabric resting on the machine.

Lower the presser foot. This *must* be done.

Bring the underneath thread up to the surface of the fabric. If the thread is left under the fabric as in normal stitching, it may get knotted with the first few stitches and cause the thread to break. Lower the needle into the fabric before starting to work.

Practise first with straight stitching: moving the hoop *slowly* in any direction, try to write your own name. Change to zig-zag stitch and work a leaf or fish shape. Fill in some spaces almost solid by moving across the shape in varying directions. Lay a piece of wool on the fabric and zig-zag over it.

The straight stitching is known as seeding and can be used either to create open spaces or to create a textured effect, when it is called closed seeding because the stitches are made very close together.

As your skill improves use layers of coloured net to give tone to your designs and incorporate other threads of varying thicknesses. These may either be tacked down first or guided with a finger as you proceed to stitch over them.

An interesting exercise is the making of Christmas Cards, where the machine embroidery is held behind a 'window'. Organdie is ideal fabric for this purpose.

The finishing touches

Stretching puckered or distorted work

If work has become stretched or distorted it is often possible to stretch it back to shape. Lay several sheets of damp blotting paper over layers of newspaper on a clean drawing board and fasten down. Place the embroidery right side up on top of the blotting paper.

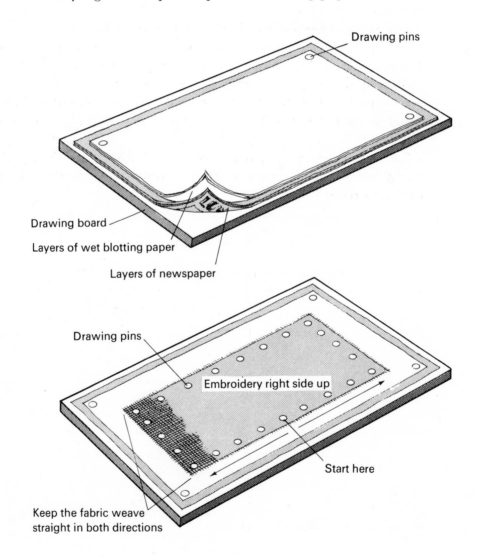

Drawing pins

Drawing board

Layers of wet blotting paper

Layers of newspaper

Drawing pins

Embroidery right side up

Start here

Keep the fabric weave straight in both directions

Starting from the middle of one side, pin the fabric down to the board; do exactly the same on the opposite side keeping the drawing pins in line. Repeat the process on the remaining two sides making sure that the weave of the fabric is lying straight in both directions. Continue pinning the fabric to the board until all the fabric is stretched and securely fastened down and is as flat as is possible.

Cover the whole work with a clean cloth and place a heavy, evenly distributed weight on top; leave for about twenty-four hours. When the embroidery is unpinned it should be flat and smooth. If your embroidery features raised effects, then the heavy weights should not be used but the embroidery should be left to stretch for a longer period.

Pressing embroidery

RAISED SURFACES—padded satin stitch, couching, braiding, Italian quilting, etc. should be pressed on the wrong side over several thicknesses of a soft piled towel.

FELT —should not be pressed. If it is creased, stretch dry directly on to a board and leave for twenty-four hours.

BEADED AND SEQUINED FABRICS—should not be pressed. Stretch dry directly on to a drawing board.

EDGES —scalloped and decorative edges are first pressed from the wrong side out towards the edges. Turn the work over to the right side, cover with tissue paper and lightly press.

FRINGES OR TASSELLED EDGES—these are not pressed. They should be hung for a while to allow the threads to fall into position. Most other forms of embroidery are best pressed from the back over a pad of soft towelling.

Mounting

Wall panels and appliqué need firm, flat mounting; for this a piece of thin hardboard or chipboard can be used. It is cut to a size which is slightly smaller than the background fabric. If the work is to be framed, then leave an extra 3 or 6 mm all round to allow for the edge to slip under the frame. The edges of the board should be rubbed down to make them smooth. Cover the board with a soft backing cloth and stick the edges of the cloth down to the back of the board.

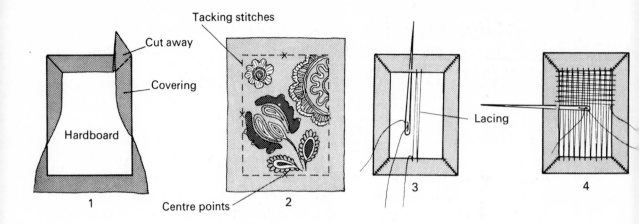

Measure the sides and mark the centres on the board. Lay the board over the embroidery and mark where the four corners come. Remove the board and with small tacking stitches outline where the board will come on the embroidered fabric. Mark the centre of the four lines.

Lay the embroidered work face downwards on the table and put the covered board in position upon it, matching the edges to the tacked lines. Match up the corresponding centre points, bring the edges of the work over the board and pin the centres of the top and the bottom, then pin the centres of the sides. Complete the pinning along the top and the bottom, pulling slightly to tighten the fabric, and then do the same at the sides.

Use an ordinary sewing needle, threaded with a very long strong thread. Start from the centre, and working outwards towards the corners, lace across the back, first from top to bottom and then from side to side. Mitre and stitch the corners, cutting away the surplus fabric.

For wall hangings use deckchair canvas or strong sail cloth as an interlining. Cut the interlining to the required size, bring the edges of the work over to the back and herringbone or catch stitch down to the interlining. Cover this with a soft lining, turn in the edges and slip stitch for a neat finish.

Appendix I
Examination techniques

Course work

You will be asked to produce course work which you have worked over a period of two or more years. You should try to make this work as varied as possible, showing that you have a wide knowledge of embroidery. Keep a loose-leaf notebook to mark the progress of your course work. Each page should show something definite, for example the experiments with fabrics before making the final choice, the cost of the chosen fabric, what sort of fibre it is made of, and the experiments with needles and threads. Make a note of all these and keep each one on a separate page. This notebook should be quite different from your class notebook which usually is not needed for assessment. The course work notebook is not necessarily a thick file but the contents must be worthwhile and must convey to the assessor what you cannot tell her in person: the build-up to the final design, what influenced your choice of colours, and any problems which you encountered and overcame.

When two or more pieces of course work are asked for, each one should be completely different in fabric, style, techniques and approach. They do not have to be of equal size: the kind of embroidery which interests you most could be the largest and the other pieces could be smaller if you wish. Your notebook will help to explain any difficulties you found and how you adapted your knowledge.

Individual study or topic

This is meant to be very much a personal effort. If possible choose a topic which is a different kind of embroidery from the work which you are going to submit as course work. A small study in depth is much more valuable than one showing large quantities of copied text; in most cases the examiner will know exactly where you have copied it all from and will know that it is not original thinking. A good study will show the planning, giving the ideas which were developed as well as those which were discarded, the selection and arrangement of material, and any points of interest or difficulty which arose during the study.

One of the most common errors is to take too wide a field, for example, 'embroidery through the ages'. If you look on the shelves of the library you will find several volumes devoted to this theme, so it is silly to think you could get all this information into a small study. Often a study can be backed up with practical illustrations as well as the written text, and the presentation will always reflect the pride of the candidate in her work.

The written examination

Read the rules and take to the examination exactly what you are told to take.

Read the whole paper through first, (time will have been allowed for this,) then read through again. The second time you should underline the important point in each question, so that when you come to write down your answer this point will be obvious to you. Note the time you have available and the number of questions you will have to answer. Note if you have to answer all of the questions or if you have a choice. Make sure that you answer only the number which you are required to do.

It is important to understand that an examiner works to a set scheme of marking. If a question asks for an explanation of four different terms, then an equal number of marks will have been given for each point. If the question asks 'Explain with the help of diagrams how ——' etc., so many marks will be given for a clear explanation and so many for clear diagrams illustrating the process.

It is essential to answer each question simply and directly. Many candidates think it will help them to gain marks if they show the examiner what they know regardless of whether it answers the question or not, but they are quite mistaken. What is irrelevant to the question is usually struck out by the examiner.

If you are asked 'What is the difference between . . .', begin your answer with 'The difference is . . .' and then put the answer simply and clearly; the examiner does not want to hunt through a lot of 'waffle' for what could be said in one sentence.

If you do not know the answer to a question, move on to the next one. Do not waste valuable time worrying about it. You may well have time left at the end when you can look again at those questions you have missed.

If the question asks for a list, make a list and do not write sentences.

In most papers there is a choice of questions in at least one section. Make sure that you know how many to answer. If you answer more than the required number, only your first answer will be considered, and you will have wasted valuable time.

If you are asked to design, do your rough sketches round the edge of the design sheet.

Take a threaded needle with you to the examination room so that if you are asked to draw the method of making a certain stitch you can then use the threaded needle in much the same way as instruments are used in Maths: that is for accuracy. Always show the position of the needle when drawing stitches; it is an important part of the process.

Finally read through your answers again before handing in your paper, and make sure that your examination number is in the correct place on the front of the paper.

The practical examination

In the practical examination you will have prepared your design in the period allowed for this, so that the second part of the examination is for showing your skill.

It is important that your design should answer the question. Read the instructions carefully and make sure that you understand what is required before putting pencil to paper or thread to fabric. Your design should be such that it fills the required area, leaving a clear margin all round to allow for the mounting and finishing.

Do the roughs for your design round the edge of the design sheet so that the examiner can see the progress of your ideas; you will not be there to tell her, and this is the only way you can let her know what you had in mind.

Colour small sections of the design and mark in the stitches you will be using; there is no need to colour or fill in the whole design with stitches.

When you start sewing try to work a small section of each part of the design, so that if the work is not completed in the time, the examiner will know the extent of your knowledge.

Do not rush your work; quality is more important than quantity. Take special care with the beginnings and endings.

Now that you have read about examination techniques, it will have become obvious to you that you will need practice in all sections of the requirements, and indeed this is the only way to be successful.

Appendix 2
Some questions from recent examinations

Theory

1 What do you understand by 'tone'? Give examples of how 'tone pattern' can be achieved.

(*Metropolitan Regional Examinations Board*)

2 Describe clearly three different ways in which embroidery designs may be transferred to fabrics and explain why these methods are used. Name a suitable material for each.

(*Associated Examining Board*)

3 Describe in detail the uses of the following in embroidery:
   (a) a crewel needle
   (b) a stiletto
   (c) an embroidery frame
   (d) French chalk

(*Metropolitan Regional Examinations Board*)

4 (a) What is the difference between 'Stranded' embroidery thread and 'Coton à Broder'?
   (b) Name three other types of embroidery thread.

(*East Midland Regional Examinations Board*)

5 Draw and name a stitch suitable for each of the following:
   (a) filling in a small area
   (b) working in a smooth line
   (c) giving a rough texture
   (d) edging.

(*Metropolitan Regional Examinations Board*)

6 Illustrate how the edges of applied shapes may be treated to achieve different effects and be suitable for different fabrics and purposes. Hand and machine stitchery can be used to show these edges

softened, merged, delineated sharply, extended or contained. Add brief explanatory notes.

(*Associated Examining Board*)

7 What is a template? With the aid of clear sketches show *three* different ways in which templates can be used.

(*City and Guilds of London Institute*)

8 State briefly the difference between Italian and English Quilting.

9 Write a brief description of the processes involved in making patchwork. Sketch *three* typical patterns and indicate how they would repeat. Why is a knowledge of patchwork of practical use to an embroidress?

(*City and Guilds of London Institute*)

10 Describe the method you would use for stretching and mounting a piece of embroidery.

(*Metropolitan Regional Examinations Board*)

Design and practical

1 Design some machine or hand embroidery to decorate a kaftan or a $\frac{3}{4}$ length tunic to be worn with trousers for evening wear. A firm rich-looking material (perhaps a furnishing fabric) would be the right basis for this embroidery. Its colour and the treatment of the decoration is left to you. Show on sketches the shape of the tunic and the position of its decoration. After experimenting, develop one idea and carry out an interesting part of the design at the practical test.

(*Associated Examining Board*)

2 Using squared paper, design a border pattern to decorate a tablemat in counted thread stitches. Measurements: 30 cm × 45 cm.

(*West Yorkshire & Lindsey Regional Examining Board*)

3 From an everyday object, e.g. the handle of a jug, the tread on a motor tyre, a window from an ancient building, draw and embroider a design suitable for use as a border on the narrow sides of a tray cloth.

(*Metropolitan Regional Examinations Board*)

4 Design a border for a cushion or a door curtain using the shape of a lollipop as a repeat motif. What stitches would you use for added interest?

5 Design and work a wall panel finished size 45 cm × 30 cm, choosing as your subject:

Top of the Pops, *or* Clocks *or* Seeds.

(Metropolitan Regional Examinations Board)

6 (a) Draw a simple motif to fit into a shape $13\frac{1}{2}$ cm × 9 cm.
   (b) Enlarge this so that the longest side measures $16\frac{1}{2}$ cm.
   (c) Reduce it so that the longest side measures $7\frac{1}{2}$ cm.
        It is important that all your constructional lines should be left showing.

(Based on a question set by City and Guilds of London Institute)

7 Make a design for a circular coffee tray-cloth, 35 cm in diameter. The design should recognise the shape of the tray and arise from the use of material and stitchery.

(Based on a question set by City and Guilds of London Institute)

8 Design an appliqué panel for the front of an altar of any denomination. Submit with your design as much as possible of the actual production of the central motif of your theme.

(Welsh Joint Education Committee)

9 Design and make an embroidered picture in materials and stitchery on *one* of the following subjects:
   (a) a fantastic animal
   (b) a doll's house
   (c) insects and foliage.

(Welsh Joint Education Committee)

10 Using three or more different kinds of string, make a wall hanging of your own choice. The string should be of different qualities and textures. The use of beads, shells, etc. for added interest is allowed.

(Metropolitan Regional Examinations Board)

11 Plan and work a motif approximately $12\frac{1}{2}$ cm high, based on *one* of the following:
   (a) a fruit or a vegetable
   (b) a crab or a shell
   (c) a church.

It is to be worked in any method of embroidery which depends for its main effect on counted threads. Outline stitches may be used, but these should be kept to the minimum. Work the embroidery in two contrasting colours only.

(Based on a question set by City and Guilds of London Institute)

12 Cut through a flower or a fruit. Draw what you see and turn it into a design to decorate any article of your own choice.

(Metropolitan Regional Examinations Board)

13 Make a simple design using paper cut-outs which could be used to decorate a bedspread. The motif to be appliquéd. Show by means of a sketch how the motif would be used.

(Metropolitan Regional Examinations Board)

14 Using the emblems of one of the apostles draw a design suitable for use on a church kneeler. What material and thread would be suitable for the work?

(Metropolitan Regional Examinations Board)

15 Design the face of a cloth doll. Show clearly the embroidery stitches you would use to obtain the best effect.

(Metropolitan Regional Examinations Board)

16 Design and work a centre panel suitable for a baby's christening robe.

(East Anglian Examinations Board)

17 Design and work a bridal coronet, to hold a bridal veil.

(East Anglian Examinations Board)

18 Design and work as much as possible of an embroidered picture or wall hanging to be given a title such as:
'Sea-shore', 'Machinery', 'Discs', 'Space', etc.

(South East Regional Examinations Board)

19 Plan and work a corner design suitable for a linen place-mat in either a traditional form of embroidery such as hardanger or cross-stitch or a modern design based on vegetables or fruit.

(South East Regional Examinations Board)

20 Using chimney-pots as a theme, make a wall hanging with a finished size of 45 cm × 35 cm.

(Metropolitan Regional Examinations Board)

Further reading

100 EMBROIDERY STITCHES (*Coats Sewing Group, Anchor Embroidery Stitches*)

BASIC DESIGN: THE DYNAMICS OF VISUAL FORM (*Maurice de Sausmarez, pub. Studio Vista,. 1969*)

OXFORD BOOK OF FLOWERLESS PLANTS (*F. H. Brightman and B. E. Nicholson, pub. Oxford University Press, 1966*)

NEEDLEWEAVING (*Edith John, pub. Batsford, 1970*)

HISTORICAL NEEDLEWORK (*Margaret H. Swain, pub. Barrie & Jenkins, 1970*)

EMBROIDERY, A FRESH APPROACH (*Alison Lilley, pub. Mills & Boon, 1964*)

CREATIVE STITCHERY (*Dona Z. Meilach and Lee Erlin Snow, pub. Pitman, 1971*)

MAKING FABRIC WALL HANGINGS (*Alice Timmins, pub. Batsford, 1970*)

PATCHWORK (*Averil Colby, pub. Batsford, 1958*)

EMBROIDERY DESIGN (*Enid Mason, pub. Mills & Boon, 1970*)

DESIGN IN EMBROIDERY (*Kathleen Whyte, pub. Batsford, 1969*)

INTRODUCING MACHINE EMBROIDERY (*Ira Lillow, pub. Batsford, 1967*)

BEAD EMBROIDERY (*Joan Edwards, pub. Batsford, 1966*)

FASHION BEAD EMBROIDERY (*Natalie Giltsoff, pub. Batsford, 1971*)

SYMBOLS OF THE CHURCH (*Ed. Carroll E. Whittemore, pub. Hodder and Stoughton, 1964*)

SAINTS, SIGNS AND SYMBOLS (*W. Ellwood Post, pub. S.P.C.K., 1964*)

ECCLESIASTICAL EMBROIDERY (*Beryl Dean, pub. Batsford, 1958*)

CHURCH NEEDLEWORK (*Hilda M. Hands, pub. The Faith Press, pub. 1920*)

CELTIC ART: THE METHODS OF CONSTRUCTION, *Books 1–6* (*George Bain, pub. William Maclellan, 1944*)

Leaflets on all kinds of embroidery can be obtained from The Embroiderers' Guild, 73 Wimpole Street, London, WIM 8AX.